The Kids' Magazine

Author & Illustrator: Derin Ayvaz

Editor: Selin Ayvaz

Publisher: Book Printing AE

Website: www.derinayvaz.com
E-mail: info@derinayvaz.com

Contents

Dedications

To my Dad

Acknowledgements

I want to thank my friend, Mira Midani, for giving me name ideas for the characters in my book. I'm so happy to have her support. Mira Midani also edited some parts of my story and I am eternally grateful for her contributions and feedback. My lovely friend, Luciana Jimenez, wanted to print and publish my story, but I couldn't let her because it needed adult approval first. However, I thank her very much for her willingness to help.

This story is based on a real person, but it's not about a real event. Inspired by my beloved fourth-grade teacher, Miss Jessica Bailey Fenwick. Her real parents are Miss Kelly and Mr. Chris. But her mom isn't bad in reality; she is really nice. And her brothers Connor and Brent are also real. Oh, and don't forget, Hailey, her cousin, is also real. Some parts of this story are real.

In writing, we had personal narratives, and Miss Bailey wrote hers. And the things that happened in real life before are contained in the chapters: Green To Gray House and Evil Snow Chaos. Miss Bailey was really happy. I started writing in class, but it wasn't an assignment. I just wanted to randomly do it because I love writing. Once, Miss Bailey saw me, and she asked, "What is going on here?" I said, "I created a book about you". She read it, and she was so happy and proud. Miss Bailey was pregnant, and terrible news came out about her baby. But that didn't stop her. She was still so proud of herself, but I was kind of sad Miss Bailey wasn't here to see me finish my book. This was the whole story of how I published my book.

Once I had a library class, and our librarian told us that our principal had written and published a real book before. So my friends asked me if they could join my book. And I said "sure". I wondered, other than an illustrator, publisher, and author, what else is there? So I went to Mr. Gilmour's office (principal) to ask him, and he asked why. I said because I'm writing a book. He looked impressed. A few days later, I saw him at the cafeteria. I said I'm the author, and my book is almost done. He said, "can't wait to see it". He might maybe publish it in the school library or something. Then I hurried up to finish my book and sent an e-mail to Mr. Gilmour. He wrote me back, and I delivered a copy of my book to his office. Anyway, I would also like to give credit to the book, "Billionaire Boy" by David Walliams. I love his series so much that his books motivated me to create a funny book.

About The Author

Derin, a vibrant fifth grader at Dubai American Academy in the United Arab Emirates, As the Elementary School President, she proudly represents students from KG-1 to Grade 5. With a keen interest in the performing arts, she has been exploring stage arts and playing the piano since the age of six. Derin is also an active athlete, enjoying volleyball and tennis, and sailing. Her adventurous spirit has even led her to become a Level-3 RSA youth sailor and sparked a new passion for windsurfing. Her enthusiasm for writing has blossomed early; at just 10 years old, she has authored her first book, marking the beginning of her exciting journey in literature. Derin's passion for reading and writing shines through her work, inviting readers into her imaginative world.

Haunted House
Chris Mitchell Prison
The Moors
BANK
Bank
Church
Mini M
Dentist
Grand Statue
Bailey's Neighborhood
Supermarket
Hospital

CHAPTER: 1
Meet Bailey's Mom

It was a cold and dark night in Duluth, Georgia. Even though it was summer, a cold breeze was blowing. The next day was the first day of fourth grade, and Bailey was nervous. She looked at the stars and was just about to close her curtains–BAM! The front door slammed open and then closed again. Bailey knew who it was–the Big Lady. Her mother, Kelly, was a big, bossy lady. She didn't like Bailey's original name, Jessica Fenwick. She went to court to legally change Bailey's name to Bailey. She was stuck with the name, even though everyone still called her Jessica.

Mom had just come home from church. She was grunting, which meant she was mad about something. The stairs started shaking as if there was an earthquake. Kelly burst into Bailey's room. "Why aren't ya in bed, li'l lady?" her mother asked.

"Well, I was just closing my cu–" Bailey started.

"Well, shush, I don't care! The Judge at that church is a big, crazy guy! Well, anyway, your name is Bailey from now on. Congratulations, tell your friends. Now sleep ya, baby!"

"Sorry, Mom," Bailey replied. She tucked herself into bed and watched

watched her mother slam the door as she left–BAM! Bailey's father, Chris, was a wonderful person. He had chosen the name Jessica, but Bailey's difficult mother kept forgetting it. She realized Bailey's name was Jessica only two weeks ago! Dad worked at the church, too. He was a lawyer, which brought him a lot of money. As a lawyer, he had the authority to manage the legal name change. However, he couldn't change Bailey's name because he was a family member. The judge her mom earlier described as a crazy character was Mitchell. He was a kind judge. Bailey loved him so much! He truly cared about Bailey's family. (Of course, not Bailey's mother, though).

Brent, her youngest brother, was asleep in his little spaceship crib. At that time, Brent was one year old. Connor was bunking in his robot-themed bed. As Brent grew older, he would bunk with Connor because little Brent's room was to become a yoga studio for their mother.

Bailey's dad was working on a case involving a man named Sean Downy, who had stolen one million dollars from the bank.

Have I told you about her mom's job? Well, she's retired now. DUHHH. She used to work at the dentist as an assistant, but her interactions with patients did NOT go well. Then, she was fired and worked at the fish counter in the supermarket. At home, she would smell like rotten snapper fish because the scent never went away. Her job went on and on until Bailey's dad got a job as a lawyer. Her dad used to work at the bank, and he was promoted before he sat for the bar exam. Now he is one of the top ten lawyers in Georgia. As her mom says, "Work does not give you money because I only earn $500 a month!"

Anyway, Bailey was really thirsty and needed some milk. Maybe some cookies with it, even though it was not Christmas.

CHAPTER: 2
Milk & Cookies

Bailey tiptoed to the door and opened it. The problem with her tiny house was that the doors were so cheap they squeaked every time they moved. This one squeaked loudly as it opened—by far the squeakiest squeak she had ever heard. Then, Bailey heard Mom storming upstairs. "If only I could make it to that closet", Bailey thought. She rushed down the hall and into the closet. "Eww, what's that smell?" she whispered. She glanced to her side and saw a pile of dirty diapers and underwear. On the other side were socks and even more underwear. Oh no! She had hidden herself in the kids' dirty laundry closet - Brent's diapers, Bailey's and Connor's underwear and socks. This was not good. As she was about to open the door, she heard Mom grunting. Bailey heard her open the bathroom door because it made a slight, gentle squeak. But Mom slammed the door. Bailey ran out downstairs and rushed to the fridge. She got her special pink glass cup and a big milk carton. She poured it in and sneaked some of Brent's tiny chocolate and oat cookies. She put them on a plate, and she heard a gentle squeak. Uh oh. She put the milk carton into the fridge and the cookie box into the counter by the sink. She put her plate and the cup into a kitchen drawer and hid inside the drawer. Sadly, she was inside the sink counter. And her head bumped into a pipe.

"FILTHY CHILDREN! FILTHY HOUSE! FILTHY LIFE!" Mom screamed. "THAT FILTHY BATHROOM SHOULD BE WORKING

BY NOW!" She screamed and stomped so loud that some glasses crashed. "EURGHH! I BETTER SLEEP BEFORE THIS FILTHY HOUSE GETS CRUNCHED!" And she stormed up the stairs. Bailey quickly drank her milk and ate her cookie. On her last bite, the doorbell rang. Mom was asleep; Bailey could tell because of her loud snoring.
She whispered, "It's open."

Dad opened the door. "Jess? What are you doing awake?" he asked.

"My name's Bailey now, according to Mother," she replied.

"Mitchell and I have thrown Sean Downy into prison," Dad exclaimed.

"Congrats, Dad," Bailey replied as she frowned and dropped her head.

"I'm sorry about your mother," Dad said.

"For now, I'm calling her Kelly! I want to act as if I'm not related to her." She responded.

"Now, don't say that, Bailey. Tomorrow, you can bike to school with Hailey. But now it's time for bed." Dad tucked her in, and it felt better than tucking herself in. Bailey quickly slept, but before sleeping, she checked her watch. 11:30 pm. She gasped. Her sleep time was really at 9:00, and it had been close to 3 hours. She couldn't believe it! So, she closed her eyes gently and fell fast asleep.

CHAPTER: 3
Hailey & Bailey

It was morning, and the sun was brighter than Bailey's smile. She opened her curtains, but the sunlight was too strong. She squinted and closed them quickly. She rushed downstairs and sat on the wooden stool. Brent was next to her in his blue high chair. And Connor was playing with his model planes. "Whoosh, vroom! Bam bam bam!" Connor was obviously playing fighter planes.

Bailey looked over at Brent, who began to cry. "Shh shh shhhh," she shushed. Mom placed carrot, cucumber, and a baby bottle on Brent's high chair table. Brent giggled. Mom placed some chocolate pancakes with chocolate milk for Bailey and Connor.

Soon, Dad came downstairs. He was wearing a black suit with a white pocket. He had black, shining, bright shoes and a brand new, clean briefcase. "Wow, Daddy! Why are you so boyish?" asked Connor. Boyish is what Connor says for manly, professional, and fancy.

"Well, I am going to a business meeting in a hotel. Also kids! Tomorrow is my brother's wedding, so you will skip school," Dad informed. Bailey smiled at the thought. She finished breakfast, brushed her teeth, and wore her backpack and uniform. She biked through her backyard, a little forest, another backyard, and then through Hailey's back door. She rang the doorbell. Hailey opened it.

"Hi Bailey! Nice bike!" Hailey said.

"Thanks, Hailey," she replied. Hailey was Bailey's cousin. It was weird how Bailey and Hailey sounded the same. Although Hailey was a naughty girl, Bailey never realized it. Both of them were 9, and they were going to fourth grade at Duluth Elementary School, DES. Hailey grabbed her violet bike, and Bailey hopped onto her pink one. Together, they pedalled off to school. Bailey would later learn more about Hailey's mischievous side.

CHAPTER: 4
Green To Gray House

Here's a story about Naughty Hailey and Bailey. Bailey kicked at a loose stone on the path and sighed. There was nothing to do. She got bored, so she walked over to Hailey's house. Hailey came out. "Let's play Mud pies!" Hailey said. "Yesterday's rain made the perfect mud." And the mud had become so unique and nice. Bailey was a follower. She would follow whatever Hailey did. Hailey loved mud pies. Hailey started mushing the mud and making shapes. Of course, Bailey did the same.

"They're gonna melt." Bailey worried, poking at her creation.

"Well, let's see about that," Hailey replied. She threw her mud pie on Bailey's wall.

"Oh no, Mom's going to kill me!" the thought echoed in her head.

Bailey's house was painted a light sage green and was expensive.

"Let's wait until tomorrow so it can dry up.", Hailey suggested.

The next day, Hailey and Bailey came back to the backyard. "Quick, the shovel!" Hailey hissed. Bailey took her father's shovel and scraped the mud from the wall. Bailey did it to all the mud pies. When she looked closely, she saw a piece of mud become green. Bailey flipped the mud pie over and saw green paint scattered on the back. Bailey and Hailey ran up to Bailey's room.

Soon, they heard mowing. Bailey looked out her window. Dad was mowing the grass. "BAAAIILLEEEEYYYY!!!!!!!!" Dad screamed. Hailey ran away through the front door to her house. It was just Bailey and her father. Here's another story.

CHAPTER: 5
Evil Snow Chaos

Hailey skipped over to Bailey's house. It smelled yummy inside. Bailey's mom was making lunch! The girls tiptoed downstairs. Bailey wasn't sure they should be going down there, but Hailey didn't seem to care.

On the way, Hailey peeked into Brent's room. She gasped. There was a giant, super-cool castle right in the middle of the floor! It had bright colors and everything.
"Wow! Check it out!" Hailey rushed into the room, her eyes widening.

"Hey! Brent and Mom aren't here!" Bailey said.

"C'mon, just for a little bit," Hailey pleaded, already engrossed with the castle.

"Ok, ok, fine," Bailey relented.

Hailey was lost playing with the castle. But then, uh-oh! She tripped, and the castle went CRASH! It bumped into the diaper-changing table and knocked over the baby powder. WHOOSH! White powder flew everywhere like a giant cloud.

"WOAH! DID YOU SEE THAT?!" Hailey asked. She took the baby

baby powder and squirted it up into the ceiling. "Snow!" Hailey said. It doesn't snow in Duluth.

There was a ceiling fan on. Bailey, of course, squirted too. Then, it was again Hailey's turn. Then Bailey, then Hailey, and it kept going. Hailey squirted it, and it got stuck in the ceiling fan. The ceiling fan sent baby powder everywhere! Now it was really snowing. Baby powder was everywhere. Just as Mom was coming upstairs, she realized. "BAILEY!!!!!" She screamed. And Hailey ran away. Now, it was just Bailey and the big woman.

CHAPTER: 6
Pancake

Time for a new adventure! On the way to school, Bailey and Hailey took a shortcut through the moors. The moors were a creepy forest on the edge of the town. Nobody went there. People thought the place was scary, creepy, full of mysteries, and bringing bad luck. Everyone said it was haunted, but only at night. The trees were tall and dark, but it was morning, so they weren't too scared. Well, maybe just a little.

The moors weren't that far. They went through the moors and back to the beautiful flower field. Hailey picked up a pink and yellow daisy and placed it in her light purple basket.

They were biking down Scale Street. It's a super famous road in their town! Bailey spotted a rock on the sidewalk, but Hailey didn't. "You're so slow!" Hailey teased, speeding way ahead of Bailey. She started biking super fast. It was like she was on a Hyper Speed Ferrari.

"Careful, Hailey!" Bailey screamed. Hailey looked puzzled for a second, and then her eyes widened as she looked ahead and saw the rock.

"AAAAH!" Hailey cried out.

When Bailey blinked, Hailey was lying flat as a pancake on the floor.

Bailey looked at the pink and yellow daisy. It was still in the basket. "Are you ok?" Bailey asked, running towards the accident.

"No!" Hailey wailed, starting to cry. Bailey helped Hailey up and supported her as she stood up holding onto the back of Bailey's bike. Together, they cycled to school, but they were really slow and steady this time.

CHAPTER: 7
Pig Academy

Bailey stopped her bike in the bike parking and put Hailey's in, too. "My knee hurts!" Hailey whined. She looked down. Her knee was purple, sore, and starting to bleed.

"Hop on!" Bailey said.

"Huh? That will never work!" Hailey replied.

"It's now or never, hop on!" Hailey jumped onto Bailey's back. Bailey started wiggling around. Hailey was pretty heavy! As they walked towards the school nurse's office, Miss Lindsay came striding down the hallway. Her long heels clattered on the floor, and her long, dark hair reached down her back. She was wearing a black dress, which looked like a suit. She looked just like a mean principal. Oh, and her smile was extra creepy!

Miss Lindsay was their principal. Her real name was Lindsay Rachel Piggson. Kids used to call her Miss Pig, but she didn't like that. There was once a new girl, who didn't know her name. But she heard others say Miss Pig. So, she said, "Hello, Miss Pig!" That girl got detention for a whole month! That's why Miss Lindsay only let people use her first name now.

"You two look rather silly! Get to class immediately. I will not allow a bunch of noodles in my school! Chop chop, hurry up!" Miss Lindsay commanded.

"Sorry, Miss Lindsay. We just had a quick accident on our bikes." Bailey explained.

"Well, that's not my fault! Go, go!" She replied.

As the girls walked away to the English class, Bailey noticed Miss Lindsay heading into the cafeteria – probably to complain about the lunch food! Changing directions, Bailey headed to the school nurse.

"Welcome, welcome, fellas!" Miss Terry greeted them with a big smile. She was a wonderful, kind nurse. "How are you, girls? How is Brent? Acting naughty? Connor? Is he still cute?" Miss Terry always asked a lot of questions.

"Uh, all good, Nurse Terry!" Bailey responded.

"Well, I see a bleeding knee. You know, I can't help with bleeding parts. I only help with fevers, colds, and broken bones." Nurse said.

"But Miss Terry! You are really good at everything!" Hailey remarked.

"I know, but I am sharing my job with Dr Paine. Nobody likes a selfish person." Just then, Dr Paine walked into the room with a creepy smile. He used to work in a scary hospital called Dungeon Evil Hospital (DEH).

It was in a dark and spooky place called Dungeon Evil City (DEC), where everything was free! That's how they tricked people into coming. They got people to come to the hospital, the stores, and the haunted abandoned houses. The news said lots of people disappeared after seeing Dr Paine.

Dr Paine got super rich and then was thrown into prison. But he tricked the police and escaped seven years ago when Bailey was only two years old. And he wasn't allowed to go anywhere himself. They made him join a happy school where nothing bad could happen. They were wrong! Dr. Paine was still as evil as ever.

As he prepared to speak, his long, pointy chin stretched down like an icicle. His hair was professionally combed, and not a single string was out of place. And, his eyes were shiny and mean.

"Good morning, children." Dr Paine said in his awkward Irish accent and continued, "I see it's Hailey."

"Yes, yes…" she muttered under her breath

"I hear you would like Miss Terry to assist you today?"

"Uh, yes?" Hailey replied.

"Well, apologize because that's quite rude!" commented Dr Paine.

"HEY, DR PAINE!" Bailey chimed in. "WHAT YA DOIN? WE WANT

MISS TERRY AND WE SAID SO." Now, Dr Paine was fuming with anger.

"MISS PIGGSON! Pardon, MISS PIG! Wait no. MISS LINDSAY!" Dr Paine said.

Miss Lindsay dashed through the hallway. "Don't make me fire you!" She snapped at him.

"Sorry Pig - Lindsay. But Hailey and Bailey should be put in detention." He suggested.

"Ok. Dr Paine. Now go! Terry will do it because you wasted your time speaking!" Miss Lindsay said.

Bailey was happy for two reasons. One, Miss Terry would do it. Two, the detention teacher, Miss Bark, was so nice.

"Oh! And tell her I will lead the detention." Miss Lindsay announced.

"NOOOO!" The girls cried out.

"Miss Bark is not going to be here tomorrow." Miss Lindsay informed the girls.

"Tomorrow? But tomorrow is Friday! And it's my best friend's birthday!" Bailey said.

"Well, you won't be there until 6:30." Miss Lindsay responded. Bailey started feeling sad.

"See you later, Hailey." Bailey looked down, feeling worried.

24

"Wait! You can't just leave me here!" Hailey said, her voice filled with panic.

CHAPTER: 8
I Want To Be On Vogue Magazine!

"Hey, Daisy," BB said.

"Hi, BB," Daisy replied.

Daisy and BB were Bailey's best friends. BB's real name was Belle Bark, but everyone called her BB because her mom was Miss Bark, the detention teacher!

"So! Let's talk about my birthday, girls!" BB said.

"OMG, yes! The main colors should be purple, pink, and blue." Daisy suggested.

"Well, I can blow up purple balloons," Daisy added.

"I'll blow up blue ones!" BB declared.

"And I'll get the pink ones", Bailey said, sounding a bit down.

"What's wrong?" Daisy asked.

"Are you not coming to my amazing 10th birthday?" BB asked, sounding worried.

"I don't know, really," Bailey replied. They looked puzzled. "I'm in detention."

"But it's your first time!" Daisy responded.

"Yeah, who knows if it's going to be bad? Especially with my mom in charge," BB tried to console Bailey.

"No, no, no. I'm with Miss Lindsay. And I don't get out until 6:30.", Bailey explained.

"Everyone is leaving their houses at 5:00," BB started speaking. "Since it takes a while to get to my house, they won't arrive before 6:00. We will wait for everyone until 6:30, and then the gates close."

"Wait, maybe I can still make it! Sunshine Court is only one block away from school!" Bailey commented.

Sunshine Court was where all the fancy houses were. There were about five, and they were all huge. BB's dad worked as a businessman, and Miss Bark was a businesswoman; teaching was her part-time job. Even the mayor and the vice president lived there. The other three houses were BB's, the Simmon family's, and Lexi's. The Simmon family had two very creepy parents and five kids. Eddie, the eldest, was studying at the Oxford University. He was 20. Sally, the second child, was 16. She acted like an adult with huge nails, and was always out with her friends. Then, there were twins, Maddie and Marcus, who were both nine, BB's friends and the same age as her. Zoe, the fifth and last child, was 3, and BB was babysitting her.

Lexi was even richer than BB. She bragged all the time because her dad was the mayor's secretary, and her mom worked with the president and vice president. Oooh, Lexi had two besties, Olivia and Kylie, who were just as mean as she was. They were the most popular girls in school, and engaged in activities like:

- Making high schoolers cry.
- Making fun of people's clothing style.
- Throwing huge parties and ignoring anyone who wasn't considered "cool".
- Bullying everyone, then acting like angels when teachers were around.

Some other popular bullies included Madison, Jessica, and Vanessa. Although the two popular bully groups worked together, their classes were different from each other.

Lexi was walking towards them.

"Party, hmm?" Lexi said.

"Yeah? So what?" Daisy replied.

"So, I need you two dweebs to invite me," Lexi demanded.

"W-why?" Bailey asked.

"Because my friends are going," Lexi answered, as if it were obvious.

"Well, you're not invited!" BB said. BB really did not like Lexi due to her the pranks Lexi played at midnight.

"Geez! Chill, BB." Daisy whispered. She and Bailey had invited her friends so Lexi would get jealous.

"Well. I'm giving you two days to put me on that list!" Lexi declared.

"Ok, ok," Daisy said.

"Go away now!" BB snapped.

Lexi walked up to BB, almost nose-to-nose. "See you later, dweebs," she said, flipping her hair in BB's face before walking away.

"OW!" BB yelled.

"Well, don't worry. She didn't invite us to her epic pool party," Daisy said.

"And last year, we went to the water park. She said she invited everyone, but the truth is she left you out." Bailey added, causing BB to sigh.

Bailey looked over at Lexi. Everyone was taking photographs of her.

Yeah, that was right. Lexi was a kid model. She was going to be featured in *Vogue Magazine*. She was really pretty, with long blonde hair. She wore a pink leather skirt and a white shirt. She had a pink jacket on and a bunch of sparkly jewellery. Her high heels, which weren't allowed in 4th grade, were replaced with pink boots. Lexi's style was a typical "mean girl 2.0". Bailey wished she could have Lexi's stuff and be the one in *Vogue Magazine*. But someday, she would!

Lexi didn't know it yet, but Bailey and her friends had a surprise in store for her.

CHAPTER: 9
Suffering Hippo

"I'm not gonna live the rest of my life like this! No! How will I be in Vogue Magazine now!?" Lexi started to yell at her iPhone 14 Pro. "No, I seriously need an answer! I need the makeup! I don't care if someone named Kelly Fenwick bought it! No, I need it now! It costs a million dollars - that's how amazing it is! You don't understand! It has the newest Sephora and Dior set! No, I don't want bags. I have like a million of those. YOU HAVE TO FIX THIS!"

Bailey and her friends were laughing. BB had asked her parents for some money, and bought the new makeup set, pretending to be Kelly Fenwick, Bailey's mom. But Lexi didn't care about her family. The art teacher, Miss Frankie, was pretending to be the Vogue Magazine representative who was calling Lexi. Miss Frankie, luckily, helped them prank Lexi. She was one of those awesome teachers everyone loved.

"Thanks!" Bailey whispered. They were in the storage room, ringing Lexi with an old-fashioned telephone. Lexi was out in the hallway, screaming, and they watched her through a crack in the old door. The art class was about to start anyway.

They grabbed their backpacks from the storage room's stationery boxes and were about to leave the room. One of the boxes on top of a high shelf was open, and Bailey must have bumped into it. Her pens, pencils, erasers, markers, crayons, stickies, paper, and everything else came tumbling down. "BAM, BAM, BAM!" An old pipe connected to the maths room was broken off the ceiling for a long time. It was hanging loose from the ceiling and crashed down onto the floor. And someone must have placed it on top of the stationery boxes. The heavy metal pipe now clanged loudly as it hit the floor. The noise caused the old pendant light fixture to fall onto the floor, too. Soon, everything in the storage room was falling. Books went flying, paint cans banged on the floor, and a huge roll of paper rolled out super-fast. The noise seemed endless.

"What in the world?" Lexi muttered.

They peeked through the crack. Lexi was walking towards the storage room.

"Get your bags quick, quick, quick!" Miss Frankie hissed. She tried to open the back door of the storage room that led to the library, but it was locked. They grabbed some large boxes and hid themselves behind them.

"What happened in here?" Lexi asked, poking around the mess. She picked up the stationery boxes and looked inside. "Where is the stationery? Whatever, I don't care."

As Lexi started to walk out the door, BB sneezed loudly. "ACHOOOO!"

Lexi turned back. "Who is in here? Who's spying on me? Come out, whoever you are!" Lexi was about to go behind the boxes for the lamps.

Where were they? Meanwhile, Miss Frankie had an idea. She found a dusty, stained piece of paper and saw one of the stationery pens roll toward her. She wrote "NO STUDENTS ALLOWED" on the paper and slid it toward Lexi's feet.

Lexi felt the tap on her light pink Converse sneakers. "Eww! Is that ant poop on it? And dust? Oh no." Lexi carefully picked up a small box, the size of a book, took off her shoe and placed her bare foot on the box. She studied her shoe. It was covered in rat poop, dust, and termites. "EW, EW, EW!" She threw both of her Converse shoes at the lamp boxes. They were falling, but Miss Frankie managed to pull them back up. She found some cleaning gloves on a shelf and picked up the piece of paper.

"Ok?" she said, though she was distracted by a beetle climbing up the finger. "AAAH AAAH AHH!" Lexi screamed. She looked for something shiny object to use as a mirror, desperate to make sure none of the yucky stuff got on her face. She took her Converse shoes with the gloves and went to open the door. But when Miss Lindsay stopped her with her strong, sweaty hand, Lexi moved back to avoid getting any sweat on her new, fancy shirt from somewhere expensive.

"What are you doing in the storage room?" Miss Lindsay asked.

"I don't know. I was on a call, and I thought I heard something in there!" Lexi stammered.

"After class, my office." Miss Lindsay said. Bailey thought Lexi might try to bribe her, but Miss Lindsay might not be swayed. Lexi ran to the math class without another word.

"No running!" Miss Lindsay yelled. But, Lexi continued, heading straight to Mr. Osborne. Mr Osborne was a tall, skinny man with a big nose, bald head, and glasses. He walked with a hunched back, his eyes glued to the floor. He spoke in a voice that resembled a suffering hippo.

CHAPTER: 10
The Shine Team

It was finally November, and Bailey was so happy that she was daydreaming until someone interrupted.

"I can't take it anymore!" BB exclaimed. "I just hate that girl!"

"Everybody does," Daisy replied. It was the last period of the day: math. They walked to the math class with their bags still torn from the storage room mess.

"Okay, class. Today we're focusing on multiplication. Please get your blue numeracy notebooks and place them on your desks." Mr. Osborne announced. "Page 28. Complete the five worksheets. Then, practice your math facts on a sheet I will pass out to you. You will need to work with a partner-four people per group. Teamwork makes the dream work."

Bailey hated phrases like this. They were so UGHHHH! Lexi winked at her sassy group. Madison, Jessica, Vanessa, Olivia, and Kylie were all in a group. There were five, so not everyone could be partners. Lexi raised her hand. "I don't have a partner," she said, blinking cutely at the teacher.

"BB, Daisy, Bailey, please partner with Lexi." Mr. Osborne instructed.

"Fine," Daisy replied.

They worked diligently for about 30 minutes. When Mr Osborne chimed the bell, he said "Attention, kids! We still have 15 minutes for sharing. I hope you are done."

"We only worked for 30 minutes!" Lisa Lao exclaimed from the back of the class. Lisa Lao had joined the school two years ago from China and was known as the Miss-Know-It-All.

"Uh… I… do… wan… too… a…" Mr Osborne continued coughing so much that he was barely understandable.

"Just shush already!" Kaila Windsor snapped. Kaila was a school bully who targeted those who annoyed her. Bailey's team was the last to present their project, so they had to go to the front of the class.

"Guess what?" Lexi said, deliberately tripping Bailey over!

"Oh, Daisy, what did you do? Oh no! Did BB tell you to do it? Daisy, why did you listen to her?" Lexi asked.

"Well, girls…" Mr. Osborne began, but he was coughing too much to continue. He started wheezing and had to call Miss Lindsay for assistance because he couldn't talk.

"Poor guy, he is so old," Kaila said. Everyone in the class laughed. But Bailey, BB and Daisy remained silent. The room fell silent, the only sound the ticking of the clock on the wall.

"Daisy and BB, come to my office, please. Bailey, you come too," a voice called from outside. They didn't need to ask who it was.

"Girls, I am so… proud of you!" Miss Lindsay exclaimed. "Your grades and test scores have jumped so high!"

"But what about the project disaster?" BB asked.

"Oh, don't worry about that. It's just chaos. Anyways, I would like you three to join the Shine team." They all laughed. They were so happy with the news. "The Shine team only has five members. You are the luckiest students chosen to take over students and tell them how to be kinder and better." They were honestly super-duper happy. They squealed with excitement.

"Oh yes, and the other members are Lisa and Whitney." Miss Lindsay added.

"Great, the Miss-Know-It-All and a complete nerd," Bailey muttered under her breath. BB seemed to hear her, as she told Bailey to be grateful. So, Bailey just kept her thoughts to herself. They walked out of the office and saw Wilmadeene, their friend with the longest name in their grade. Some people called her Wilma. But she preferred Deenie. So, nobody called her Wilmadeene.

"Hey, I heard you guys are joining the Shine," Deenie said, as she approached them.

"Yeah, it could be hard to fit in as new members," Daisy replied.

BB scoffed, "With those losers?"

"What losers?" Deenie asked.

"The newbies. You know..? Whitney and Lisa." Bailey said.

Deenie chuckled as if she was making fun of them. "Ciao girls, I'm late for music," she said, laughing as she walked away.

BB rolled her eyes. "Sometimes, she can be annoying," she commented.

"Don't be rude. She's our friend. She's just joking around with us." Daisy said.

"Huh?" BB asked.

"I said she- " Daisy began but she was interrupted.

"Why are you raising your voice?" BB questioned.

"Because you couldn't hear me!" Daisy answered.

They both frowned at each other and walked away in opposite directions. Bailey pointed to her left, and they went that way so they could go to science class. This friendship was kinda challenging. Daisy was the nice girl, and BB could be mean. And Bailey had to sort things out all the time. They frequently argued!

Bailey was on her way to science class when she accidentally bumped into Kaila. Kaila looked at her with a frown. "Did you do that on purpose?" she asked in a mean tone. "Watch where you're going, loser," Kaila gave Bailey a rude smile and pushed her aside.

"No, no, I swear," Bailey replied as Kaila and a bunch of her mad friends surrounded her. Luckily, Miss Lindsay came in.

"Hey Bailey, I am ready to officially make you and your friends part of the Shine Team!" Miss Lindsay said, carrying a stack of binders and folders. Bailey struggled to keep track of everything.

"Ok!" Bailey replied, following Miss Lindsay to avoid Kaila.

Bailey was excited about joining the Shine Team, but she had a feeling it wouldn't be all sunshine and rainbows.

CHAPTER: 11
Not Booger Boy!

It was Monday morning, and Bailey was already feeling grumpy. Mondays were always her least favorite day of the week. The weekend had been so much fun! As she walked through the gates of Duluth Elementary School (DES), she was just about to put some books in her locker when Daisy came running up to her.

"Did you hear the news!? Amanda Drapen, the owner of Vogue Magazine, is opening new spots for her magazine!" Daisy said, jumping up and down excitedly.

"So what? Lexi is going to get it." Bailey replied, sounding uninterested. "No, no, no! You don't understand! Amanda is starting a fashion battle challenge for the cover because she's losing viewers to Marie Claire, another fashion magazine that's gaining popularity!" Daisy explained eagerly.

"Well, that's great! How do I sign up?" Bailey inquired, her interest piqued.

"Check out the latest magazine starring Selena Gomez. It has all the details," Daisy answered.

"Alright, I'll look into it. Thanks, Daisy." Bailey said.

"Okay, see ya!" Daisy exclaimed. They had an art class with Miss Frankie today. Bailey only knew a few of her classmates: Lisa, Deenie, BB, Madison, and Kaila. Poor Daisy was stuck with Whitney and all the popular brats.

"Today, we will be editing our self-portraits by styling clothes. Please make sure they are school-appropriate and get my approval before posting them to the ESJ." Miss Frankie instructed.

The ESJ was where they shared their schoolwork and got feedback from their teachers. There were ESJ, MSJ, and HSJ - Elementary School Journal, Middle School Journal, and High School Journal.

Bailey headed to the bathroom and ran into Hailey, chatting with her friends Gracie and Laura. Since Bailey and Hailey were the same age, she knew Gracie and Laura too, but they barely talked.

"I have science now, but obviously, I need to take a break," Hailey said. Bailey just nodded and went back to art class. In class, Madison was showing off her Versace dress drawing, Kaila had added some tattoos to hers, Deenie just kept it casual, Lisa had made a school uniform, and BB had drawn a pink dress.

Bailey looked at everyone's ideas but felt unsure about her own. She decided on a red dress with flowers and some red clips. The boys in their class were working together, and Miss Frankie had trouble keeping of whose paper was whose.

Next, they were supposed to do partner work to create a background for their characters. Guess who Bailey was paired with? Bob Shelmins, known as Booger Boy. And if you're wondering, Booger Girl is someone named Fiona Bart. But, you'll meet her later. For now, Bailey was stuck with Bob for a project that could take weeks. Bailey had the nerve to ask Miss Frankie if she could work alone, but Miss Frankie said that would be hard. Bailey even asked if she could change partners, but Miss Frankie declined that request as well. Bailey really didn't want to work with Bob. She turned back and saw Bob picking his nose. She sighed. The only thing Bailey could think of was getting into trouble to escape. She asked Daisy if she wanted to join her plan.

"Well, erm…" Daisy stammered.

"Great, let's go!" Bailey said. She went over to Mike Crotch (who was known for causing trouble) and stepped on his toe. Mike didn't snitch, but she made sure he would.

When Miss Frankie found out, all she said was, "Please go back to your seat and do what was asked." So, Bailey decided to dig in more. She grabbed a red Sharpie and drew an ugly squiggle. Since Sharpies were permanent, it was hard to clean off.

When Miss Frankie saw the mess, she was upset. "Please don't do that again! We haven't used Sharpies this year, so you might have forgotten they're permanent."

Soon then, the ASA (American Schools Association) arrived. They were visiting schools across North America to rate them. Bailey forgot they were coming to their school today. She heard a knock on the door and saw a tall woman with a straight face in a black suit. Next to her was a short, bald man in a black suit with a notebook. Miss Frankie knew what was happening and hurried to prepare. She fixed her dress and twirled her hair. Meanwhile, Bailey grabbed different colors of paint in cups and threw them all over herself.

"I'm so sorry I dropped these by accident!" she said, pretending to be shocked.

Miss Frankie looked furious but tried to stay calm. "It's fine, umm! Does anyone have a towel?" she asked, but the paint wouldn't come off. Bailey squirted a drop of water down her neck, which Miss Frankie didn't notice.

When the tall woman with the black suit came in, she looked at Bailey up and down and asked, "What is this nonsense you are wearing?"
"Oh, it's art, so I tried being creative and-" Miss Frankie stopped as she saw the bald man writing things down that the tall woman whispered into his ear.

"I am Jay Koral. Head of Elementary Schools Corporation Headquarters," the woman introduced herself. There was a pin-drop silence.

Miss Frankie explained, "This dress was made from paint, see?" She turned around, and a scream echoed through the room. She turned back to see the mess Bailey had made.

"PLEASE BE MORE CAREFUL IN THE BATHROOM, NOT THE CLASSROOM!" Jay yelled. The squirted water from Bailey's prank had created a puddle on the floor. "AAAAH!" Jay shouted again as she ran out of the classroom.

Miss Frankie closed the door and demanded, "WHO DID THIS?!" No one said anything. "TELL ME NOW! Was it you, Bailey?" Now Bailey was truly scared. "Off to the principal's office now!" Bailey grabbed her bag and skipped out, feeling relieved. Miss Frankie was puzzled. Luckily, Miss Bark was there that day; otherwise, she would have had to deal with Miss Lindsay, the assistant principal who was known for being strict. Miss Bark had a reputation for being stern.

"Uh oh," Bailey thought. Bailey's heart pounded as she walked into the principal's office, unsure of what awaited her.

CHAPTER: 12
The Four Fashionistas

"Miss Bark, I'm so sorry, but Miss Frankie put me with Bob Shelmins!" Bailey said.

"I don't understand why my daughter is friends with someone like him." Miss Bark replied. Bailey gulped, and she started laughing.

"I know what it's like, honey. Sometimes, you just have to deal with things you can't change. I remember when I was a kid-" Suddenly, there was a knock on the door. It was Jay Koral.

"Your art teacher really entertained me today!" Jay said. "I really loved the dress she made, especially that girl who was spilling paint on her dress for a design. I think it's so creative! Oh, there that girl is!" Bailey was overjoyed. Miss Bark was thrilled too. Once Jay left, Miss Bark screamed with joy.

"Thank you so much, love. So, you want to be on Vogue?" Miss Bark asked Bailey.

"Yeah…" Bailey replied.

"Oh, well, good for you!" Miss Bark said. "I'll email Miss Frankie to change your partner and let her know you made Miss Jay proud."

"Okay! Thanks, Miss Bark!" Bailey said.

"You are off to go!" Miss Bark said as she dismissed Bailey.

The next day, Bailey had a music class with Hailey. She was excited but suddenly remembered she had forgotten her saxophone! Miss Violet, the music teacher, began the class. "Let's start with warm-ups," she said. "Eeee aaaa aaaaaaaaaa num num num num diagram and…" The class followed along with warm-up exercises.

"Alright, next! Mi mo ma mi mu mi mo ma mi mi mo ma mi mu mi mo ma mi mu mi ma mo muuuuu. Now, let's move to the next octave and…" After the warm-ups, Miss Violet instructed everyone to get their instruments. Bailey felt her hands shaking with nerves. She knew that if she forgot her saxophone, she would lose a mark, and three marks would lead to a bad grade.

Lexi, who was also in the music class and had chosen a saxophone, had a special deal with Miss Violet. She had given her some extra money so that if she ever forgot her saxophone, she could make up for it five times!

"Lexi!" Bailey whispered. "Can I please have your saxophone?" she asked.

Lexi looked at Bailey strangely, then enquired, "Well, well, well. Look who forgot her instrument. Did you lose it, or did your mommy forget to pack it for you?"

Bailey replied with a little embarrassment. "Just let me borrow yours, please? I'll do anything!"

"Well, no." Lexi refused.

"Please, I'm on my second mark!" Bailey pleaded.

"Anything? Fine! You have to give me your lunch money and dance in the middle of the Middle school hallway!" Lexi responded.

Bailey thought about it and decided she couldn't risk a bad grade. "Okay, deal," she agreed.

Lexi handed her the saxophone, and Bailey raised her hand. "Can I go clean it, please?" Bailey asked.

"Sure, but don't take long. You should have done it before class." Miss Violet said.

Bailey cleaned the saxophone and thanked Lexi. Lexi rolled her eyes at her, and Miss Violet handed Lexi a maraca to play with.

After music class, they had math again with Mr. Hippo. Bailey remembered she had a Shine team meeting that day. She hoped it would be during math class so she could skip some time with Mr. Osborne.

Twenty minutes into the lesson, while working on their workbooks for the upcoming test, Miss Lindsay knocked on the door. "Bailey Fenwick?" she asked.

"Yes, that's me…?" Bailey replied nervously.

"Please come with me to the principal's office." Bailey felt scared and gulped. Everyone was looking at her curiously.

She was too shy to say this, but she did. "W-W-Why?" she asked.

"Just come, please!" Miss Lindsay insisted.

Bailey slowly walked out of the room, picked up her backpack, and followed Miss Lindsay down the hall. Is it about the Shine Club meeting? she wondered. But BB was in math class too, and she hadn't been called. Bailey sat down in a chair and looked around. There was Miss Lindsay, Miss Bark, and four women. One had long blonde hair, a pink headband, and a pink dress that looked very expensive. Another had brown hair and wore a sparkly shirt, black flared pants, and a black jacket. The third had pink hair that looked bleached several times, a red dress with matching red high heels and a beautiful Louis Vuitton bag. The last had short red hair, a lot of makeup, a black dress, and long black boots. Bailey was so confused. Who were these fashionistas?

"I'm Tina Sones, a model from the United States, and I work at Vogue Designer Models headquarters," the blonde woman said.

"My name is Valeria Lutya. I am a model from Russia, and I work with Tina," the brown-haired one added.

"I'm Arella Motino. I'm the head model and designer," said the woman with pink hair.

Finally, the red-haired woman spoke, "I'm Mia Sachare, a makeup artist and model from Italy. I work with them."

"And you know me already," Miss Bark added. "Remember yesterday when you told me you wanted to try out for the kids' Vogue cover magazine? I was so happy about the news Miss Jay shared, and I knew it was because of you. So, I wanted to thank you for this."

"Thank you so much!!!" Bailey said excitedly.

"I already contacted your mom to let her know you'll be home late today. But after your Shine team meeting, can you come back here?" Miss Bark asked.

"Sure," Bailey replied.

CHAPTER: 13
A Mushy Meal

The Shine team meeting was held in a huge club area on the first floor. Sadly, Miss Frankie was hosting, and it was obvious that she wasn't pleased with Bailey. She barely spoke to Bailey throughout the meeting, leaving BB and Daisy to do all the talking.

"Welcome to the first Shine team meeting! How is everybody? Good? Do you guys think we should have more members?" BB and Daisy asked. Everyone agreed, and Bailey just nodded.

"According to my calculations, adding more kids might make some people jealous, so if we just-" Lisa Lao started, but was interrupted by Whitney.

"I want moreee!" Whitney said.

"Alright then, let's make posters and put them around the school to inform people to meet me in my room. Alright, we're done. See you next time." Miss Frankie dismissed the meeting. Bailey thought about leaving the Shine team. It seemed so boring. What if they ended up with even worse people in the club?

On Wednesday, they started putting up the posters. Here's how they made the posters:

The handwriting was awful, thanks to Whitney. And the logo was pretty ugly because Lisa designed it.

The new members began arriving. First came Bob Shelmins, who was throwing a booger around. Then came Fiona Bart, picking her nose. Are you kidding me? Bailey thought to herself. Three boys who looked like triplets followed. Deenie walked in happily with her notebooks. And then Kaila showed up while grinding her knuckles into Oliver, a school nerd. And apparently, Oliver and Kaila were both in the club. Lexi, Kylie, and Olivia walked in next, flipping their hair. Finally, Marcus came in asking, "Where's Maddie?"

"Unfortunately, she didn't make it or pass the test." Miss Frankie replied.

"Our meetings will be every Tuesday, Wednesday, Thursday, and Friday. So Monday is a day off," she added. The meeting today was just an introduction, so nothing interesting happened.

As Bailey was leaving the club room, she realized it was time for lunch, the worst part of the day. Sitting down at the cafeteria table with her friends (BB, Daisy, Deenie, and Maddie), she opened her lunch bag slowly, hoping she'd packed lunch. "NOOOO!" She yelled.

"What's wrong?" Maddie asked.

"My mom only packed snacks for me and no lunch!" Bailey complained.

"Well, good luck with Miss Mush. Hopefully, she doesn't have the blue chicken special today!" Maddie joked.

Deenie laughed. Miss Mush was the lunch lady with a big smile who invented her own recipes. The problem was, her food didn't taste very good. She mixed sticky tack with mashed potatoes. Honestly, Bailey wasn't even sure if it was edible. Miss Mush made a lot of fish cakes, which Bailey didn't like much. The blue chicken was apparently a special, but Bailey couldn't imagine why anyone would want to eat a chicken that was blue.

Bailey walked over to the lunch counter with her $20 and was ready to order. She was traumatized when she saw the menu.

She really didn't want any of it, but she was starving. "Five pieces of fudge piles, orange juice, one apple, and… Can you make a sandwich?" Bailey asked.

"No, we're out of bread. But we do have gluey gummy bears and slimy rice surprise if you're interested," Miss Mush replied with a wide smile.

"Blue chicken, but not blue?" She inquired again.

"I can't change it." Miss Mush replied.

"How about mashed potatoes, but can you leave out the tacks?" Bailey requested.

"What about fish cake? They're extra crispy today," Miss Mush suggested, holding up a tray of weird-looking fish cakes.

"Umm, no, thank you. Maybe just some rice," Bailey said.

"Ok, your total is $26." Miss Mush said.

Bailey's tummy felt like it was full of butterflies. She quickly looked through her purse, hoping to find some extra money. "Uh oh," she whispered as she realized she did not have enough! "I'm six dollars short!" What should she do? She looked at BB with worried eyes, hoping her friend could help. She kindly gave it to her. Bailey went back to Miss Mush and paid.

"Thank you," Bailey said.

Bailey gave one fudge pile to each of her friends. They were chocolate cakes shaped like poop, but they tasted good. Bailey finished up her orange juice and ate her rice and mashed potatoes.

CHAPTER: 14
Fashionista 5 (Bailey)

After the Shine Club meeting and lunch, Bailey returned to Miss Bark's office. The four models were waiting for her. They led her outside to a sleek black limo, complete with disco lights, a bed, a bathroom, couches, a TV and bottles of champagne.

"Champagne?" Mia asked, holding a glass of apple juice.

"Yes, please!" Bailey replied. As the limo drove to Vogue Designer Model Headquarters (VDMH), Bailey gazed out the window and noticed that a man in a black suit was there.

"This is the bodyguard, Mitch," Tina introduced the man.

Walking inside, Bailey was so amazed by the sight. There were golden necklaces and Versace dresses on almost everybody. There were mini designer stores and mini makeup shops. There was a humongous makeup studio and an impressive longue next to it. They went inside the lounge. Through a tiny window, Bailey gasped as she spotted the real Ariana Grande getting her makeup done in the studio! She couldn't believe her eyes. So many celebrities were passing by everywhere. How had Bailey's mom allowed her to experience something like this? Anyway, Bailey didn't know, but she was grateful.

"Bailey Fenwick?" A British voice called out. Bailey followed Mia into the makeup studio. Mia was a makeup artist. She put Bailey's hair into a bun and put some makeup on her face. Then, Arella led her to the dress-up room, where Bailey was given a pretty sparkling pink dress and a matching pink diamond clip for her hair. The dress and accessories seemed incredibly expensive. Arella styled Bailey's hair beautifully and handed her a pink handbag from a designer store. Finally, Bailey was given pink tap-dancing shoes.

Valeria then brought Bailey to the photo-shooting room. Afterward, all four fashionistas brought her to a room labelled 'Contest Room'. Kids in high-fashion outfits were lined up everywhere. It was clear that entering this contest was not cheap. Guess who Bailey saw? Lexi! She was looking even more glamorous than she felt.

There were 100 kids competing in the contest, with 13 rounds to determine who would be on the cover. In the first round, they did catwalks, and ten kids were eliminated. The next round involved hair flips, and another ten kids were cut. The process kept going until only 50 kids remained.

After a one-hour break, Bailey fell asleep in the lounge. When she woke up, she checked the time, and realized the contest would be starting in 30 minutes! Bailey was thirsty, so she ran to the door, but it was locked. Bailey's heart pounded as she then realized she was trapped. Would she make it to the contest in time?

CHAPTER: 15
The Last Round...

Bailey was sure that Lexi was behind the locked door. After all, who else could it be? She was all alone in the lounge except for the orange fish in a big fish tank. She was stuck with no quick way. Desperate, she decided to go with Plan A: scream for help.

"AAAAAAAAAAAHHH HELP MEEEEEE!" Bailey yelled. But, nobody heard her. The contest room was full of noise. Lexi had cleverly closed the curtains, so Bailey could not see outside. What was she gonna do? It seemed like Lexi had set her up to fail. Bailey felt really sad and worried that Lexi might win the cover. She just had to wait and hope for the best.

Bailey waited for what felt like a really long time. She was starting to think she was imagining things when she heard a knock on the door. She was probably hallucinating. She tried to make sure she wasn't, so she slapped cheek to cheek. "Help, please!" she shouted. The door opened, and it was Tina.

"What are you doing here? The contest starts again in 1 minute!" Tina asked, surprised to find Bailey locked in the lounge.

"Someone locked me in here, and I bet it's Lexi!" Bailey explained herself urgently.

"Alright, come with me. I'll talk to the judge." Tina said, taking Bailey by the hand. They hurried to the contest room, where Bailey quickly took her place back on the stage. Tina approached the judges, whispering in their ears.

The contest continued with a lot of excitement and thrilling challenges, including a dance-off, a talent show, and a question-and-answer competition about fashion history! Audience held their breath with each new task. After several rounds, only five contestants were left. The focus was now on hair, and Bailey was relieved to see that both she and Lexi were still in the running. Obviously, Lexi was getting this done. But so did Bailey! So Bailey and Lexi were the last two kids left.

The final challenge was to find out who had the better outfit. Dramatic music played, making everyone nervous. The judges looked at the contestants and their outfits. Lexi was wearing a dazzling gold dress with real diamonds, clearly a showstopper.

The Judge cleared his throat and announced, "And the winner is ..." Bailey held her breath, her heart pounding. Would the judge choose Lexi, or could Bailey's effort be enough to win?

CHAPTER: 16
Meeting The Goddess

"Jessica Fenwick!" the Judge announced.

"IT'S BAILEY!" Bailey's mom shouted from the crowd. Bailey had almost forgotten she was there.

"What in the world did you just say? You made a mistake. It's Lexi. I am Lexi, not Bailey. She is Bailey." Lexi said, looking really angry.

"You did something very wrong by locking her in the lounge. This is just getting back at you," the Judge said firmly.

"Okay, I get it. I learned my lesson. So, do I win now?" Lexi asked, sounding annoyed.

"No, you don't! Security, please help her get off the stage!" the Judge ordered. Mitch, the bodyguard, and two other security guards came and took Lexi away.

"Congratulations, Jessica. You get the cover," the Judge finally announced.

"BAILEY!!!" Bailey's mom yelled again. The four fashionistas took Bailey to the photo-shooting room, where she saw lots of celebrities all clapping for her. Lexi was peeking through the window, and her mascara was running like black paint dripping from her eyes. She looked mad-jealous. Bailey was so happy she felt like she might faint. She pinched herself and slapped her cheeks to make sure it was real. It was real, but whatever, it hurt. She walked off the stage with flowers and gifts and ran into Amanda Drapen! Amanda was probably the richest woman in Atlanta and the owner of Vogue magazine. She was in charge of everything, and no one was in charge of her.

"Congratulations, Bailey," Amanda said with a smile.

"Thanks…" Bailey replied shyly.

"I'll be happy to see you at the photo-shooting room on Friday," Amanda added.

"Okay," Bailey replied, squealing with joy. She then went to tell her friends. Her mom was driving her home.

"Mom, aren't you happy I won?" Bailey asked.

"Yeah, sure! But it would be better if you got a RICHER job. Like a Lawyer," her mom answered.

"Mom, this isn't my job forever. Chill. But I can be a model when I grow up." Bailey joked, and her mom looked at her strangely.

The next day at school, everyone was chanting Bailey's name and congratulating her. It was the best feeling ever. Bailey walked through the halls and saw BB and Daisy.

"Congratulations, Bailey. We are so happy for you. We're glad Lexi didn't get it." Daisy said.

"Yeah! It's tough to be in the Vogue." BB agreed.

"Our bestie is a model!" Daisy squealed.

"Yay!" They all cheered together.

CHAPTER: 17
Party Planning

"This isn't going to end like this," BB said.

"We need a party!" she exclaimed.

"Yeah!" Daisy agreed.

"Your photo-shoot is on Friday. We can have the party on Saturday! We will start planning now. After the photo-shoot, we can print the pictures extra large and hang them up everywhere at the party! We can invite the models if they can come, and –" BB was cut off.

"Okay, okay, chill, BB! You are freaking poor Bailey out." Daisy said. Bailey started laughing.

"Sounds good," Bailey commented.

After school, Miss Bark picked them up and drove them to the mall. BB was in charge of getting party supplies and decorations. Daisy was handling the invitation cards, hiring a DJ, and the food. And Bailey was raising money for the party and getting the photo-shoot done. She had an idea.

"What if we charge $10 for each invitation?" Bailey suggested.

"Sure!" Daisy agreed.

They knew the perfect party place: Party & Co, MEGASTORE! They went there, and BB went straight to the decorations and supplies section. Daisy looked at some cards and asked, "Should we have goodie bags?"

"Good question. We should, so everyone will be happy!" Bailey replied.

"Ok, you are the boss," BB said.

While Daisy looked at cards, Bailey went to the Party & Co Cafe. They had a café, which was so cool! Bailey asked them about party food, and they offered ten boxes of pizza, a golden customized cake, 100 mini cupcakes, and ten huge bags with mini chip bags inside.

"How much is that?" Bailey asked.

"It's our special package, which would be $1,100," the worker informed.

Bailey put on her sweetest smile and said, "Wow, this is too expensive! Any chance we could get a discount? We're throwing a big party for the whole school, and we're trying to raise money for good."

The worker's eyes widened as he recognized. "Wait, a minute," he said. "Are you …, hmm, you look like the girl who won the contest on Vogue TV!" the worker exclaimed.

Bailey nodded shyly. "I am."

"Well, it's an honor to meet you! And for such a good cause, you deserve a special discount. Would you take for $500?" the worker asked.

"Sure! Thank you so much" Bailey said gratefully. "I'll pick it up later."

Daisy found really cute cards. "Each one is $1. It's probably cheap," she said. Bailey looked at their list of people they made earlier. There were 85 people.

"Okay, so it would cost $85," Daisy calculated.

"Yeah," Bailey agreed.

Daisy bought the cards. She then wrote something, then printed it and stuck it to every card.

"I found this gold banner that says 'Congratulations.' These are gold and black balloons and random decorations like hanging stuff. It's the gold pack, and it costs $200." BB said.

"Tomorrow, let's work to get more money. I'll babysit my brothers and do chores for my parents to earn some cash," Bailey declared.

"I can babysit my neighbors, too. Since they're rich, they usually pay me $150 for 3 hours! And I'll also do chores," BB added.

"I'll do chores and… Oh, I have a cousin, Gracie. She has football practice tomorrow. I can walk her there and bring her back home. Gracie is a brat, so her parents will be happy to be away from her," Daisy said.

The next day after school, they counted how much money they raised.

"I raised $50 from chores and $100 from babysitting my brothers," Bailey announced.

"I raised $150 for three hours and another $150 for another three hours, plus $50 from chores," BB informed the group.

"I got $200 from walking Gracie and $50 from chores," Daisy said. "Let's count the money," Bailey suggested.

"$750! Not bad." Bailey said. She went and bought the food, leaving them with $250. BB used it for the gold decorations, leaving only $50. They needed $35 more for the cards.

"I'll babysit my brothers again and do the chores," Bailey said.

"Today is Thursday; the party is so soon!" BB suggested. "Try asking the teachers for some money."

Bailey found five stacks of empty sticky notes in her bag. She went to Mr. Osborne. "Can I have $35 for these sticky notes?" she asked sweetly.

"O..o..k-k-k," Mr. Osborne said, though Bailey wasn't sure what he said.

She just took the money and left.

"Okay, perfect!" Bailey exclaimed.

After school, Daisy wrote every invitation and sent them all out. While Bailey was getting her photo-shoot done, BB worked on decorating the place. They were doing it in BB's backyard. After the photo-shoot, Bailey wiped off her makeup, changed into comfy clothes, and then her mom drove her to BB's house. Bailey put the food in the fridge.

They started raising a lot of money from each invitation. They had already raised $70 from invitations. The girls were thrilled with their fundraising success, but they had no idea what surprise the party day would bring.

CHAPTER: 18
Epic Party Drama

It was Saturday morning. Daisy arrived a little late because she had to get large prints of Bailey's face from Vogue. She was busy hanging them up, while BB brought tables from inside her house to create a buffet and set up decorations. Bailey was busy counting the money. To her surprise, they had already collected $460! More people kept arriving, and the total quickly rose to $790. By the end of the day, they had raised an amazing $850!

But the surprises didn't stop there. Guests kept giving Bailey tips and money to congratulate her. One person even handed her $200! With all the tips and congratulatory money they raised, their total reached $1,490. Wow!

And then another guest donated $300, followed by $400, $500, and $200! By the evening, they had accumulated more than $3,000! Deenie arrived late to the party, but still contributed $200, pushing the total to around $3,500. Bailey could hardly believe it. "Wow! We raised so much money!" Bailey thought to herself.

The backyard was decorated with colorful lights and balloons, and a DJ played the latest pop songs. Everyone was dancing, laughing and having a great time. The party was a huge success, but they felt a bit overwhelmed by the amount of money they had raised.

"Let's donate it to charity!" Daisy suggested.

"Not all of it!" BB countered.

"Of course, but which charity?" Daisy asked. They discussed about their options.

"Kids' makeup studios!" Bailey said.

"Yeah!" BB and Daisy squealed in agreement.

Bailey continued, "I once went on a trip with my cousins to South Africa. My little cousin wanted to get her makeup done for dress-up. We went to a salon called Little Stars Makeup. It wasn't the best quality, but the workers were so nice, and my cousins loved it. Let's donate the money to them!"

"Sure! I'll just ask my mom how to do it, and the – " BB was interrupted. "Why didn't you guys invite me?" Lexi intervened.

"How did you get here?" Daisy asked, surprised.

"Let's just say you invited Deenie," Lexi said. They all looked puzzled. "What do you mean?" Bailey asked.

"I'm on her side," Deenie said as walked up.

"What?" BB asked, confused.

"I really don't like how you stole the spotlight. All Lexi wanted to do was be your friend. I don't think your mom would be too happy about this." Deenie remarked.

"Don't talk about my mom!" said Bailey.

Deenie walked up to Bailey's mom. "All Lexi wanted to do was be friends with Bailey. Your daughter has been bullying her and-"

"Deenie, I understand you might have concerns, but today is meant to be a joyful celebration for Bailey and her friends. It's important to respect their efforts and enjoy the party. Let's focus on the positive and make this a memorable day for everyone," Bailey's mom said, and Lexi started laughing.

"Wilmadeene? HAHAHAHA!" Lexi laughed.

In the end, the party was a hit, but Deenie's attempt to gain popularity by siding Lexi backfired. Nobody liked Deenie, and her efforts to stir trouble only made things worse. This is why one should be cautious about getting involved with people like Lexi.

CHAPTER: 19
Present Opening

After the party, they all cleaned up, which took a long time. They opened the presents by the fireplace on the cold, windy night. The fireplace was crackling and crunching its fire, creating a cozy and relaxing atmosphere. Miss Bark handed them hot chocolate as they opened their gifts.

"To Bailey, from Daisy," read one tag. Bailey opened the gift and exclaimed, "Aww!" Inside was a little fluffy dog plushie, with a cute golden hat that said "Congratulations!"

Then Bailey discovered something else in the gift. "A pacifier? Is it for the dog? I don't think dogs use pacifiers," she said, puzzled.

"Oh, that's for Brent," Daisy explained. Bailey laughed out loud. "I picked out this puppy because you love dogs, and I remembered how much you love your little brother," Daisy added.

"To Bailey, from BB," read another tag. Bailey opened this package, which was a bit bigger. "Wow, that's so cool!" she said as she revealed a large Barbie head with makeup supplies for customizing it. "I got you this because I know you love fashion and makeup, and I thought you'd have fun designing your own Barbie looks," BB explained.

"Thank you so much, guys!" Bailey said. "Oh, and I have something for both of you too." She handed them friendship bracelets with their initials on each heart of their colors: pink, purple, and blue. "I made these myself to show you how much I love being your friend," Bailey said, a smile spreading across her face.

"Thank you so much!" Daisy said.

"It's so cute!" BB commented. They all wore their bracelets.

"As long as we have these on, we will be besties forever," Bailey said.

Bailey felt so happy and proud. She had won the contest, helped other kids, and had the best friends a girl could ask for. She knew this was just the beginning of her amazing adventures. And that was how she became famous (Hehe). But more importantly, it was the start of a new chapter filled with fun, fashion, and friendship.